First World War
and Army of Occupation
War Diary
France, Belgium and Germany

40 DIVISION
120 Infantry Brigade
Queen's Own Cameron Highlanders
11th Battalion
9 June 1918 - 1 May 1919

WO95/2611/2

The Naval & Military Press Ltd
www.nmarchive.com
Published in association with The National Archives

Published by

The Naval & Military Press Ltd

Unit 10 Ridgewood Industrial Park,

Uckfield, East Sussex,

TN22 5QE England

Tel: +44 (0) 1825 749494

www.naval-military-press.com

www.nmarchive.com

This diary has been reprinted in facsimile from the original. Any imperfections are inevitably reproduced and the quality may fall short of modern type and cartographic standards.

© **Crown Copyright**
Images reproduced by permission of The National Archives, London, England, 2015.

Contents

Document type	Place/Title	Date From	Date To
Heading	WO95/2611/2.		
Heading	40th Division 120th Infy Bde 11th Bn Cameron High'drs Jun 1918-May 1919 Formed 1918 June.		
Heading	40th Div. 120th Bde. War Diary 11th Battn Cameron Hldrs. June 1918.		
War Diary	Etaples	09/06/1918	10/06/1918
War Diary	Les Ciry Rees	11/06/1918	21/06/1918
War Diary	La Belle Hotesse.	23/06/1918	30/06/1918
Miscellaneous	40th Div. No. 27/4/G.	22/06/1918	22/06/1918
Miscellaneous	120th Infy Bde.	22/06/1918	22/06/1918
Miscellaneous	O.C. H.B.C.D. Coy.	22/06/1918	22/06/1918
Miscellaneous	Refce Para 2.		
Heading	40th Div. 120th Bde. War Diary 11th Battn, Cameron H.l.D.R.S. July 1918.		
War Diary	La Belle Hotesse.	01/07/1918	18/07/1918
War Diary	Sercus	19/07/1918	31/07/1918
Miscellaneous	B.A.B. Trench Code No. 4.	07/07/1918	07/07/1918
Miscellaneous	9543 Lieut Bruce J.J Bruce Lt.		
Miscellaneous	The Adjt 11th Garr Cameron Hlders	10/07/1918	10/07/1918
Miscellaneous	Received from Asst Adjt Copy Of "B.A.B" No. 9546.	09/07/1918	09/07/1918
Miscellaneous	Received From Asst Adjt One Copy Of B.A.B. No. 9543.	09/08/1917	09/08/1917
Miscellaneous	120th Infantry Brigade.	09/07/1918	09/07/1918
Miscellaneous	To O.C., 11th Battn Cameron Highlanders. Through Hd. Qrs. 120th Infantry Brigade.	14/07/1918	14/07/1918
Miscellaneous	120th Infy. Bde. No. 120/443.	23/07/1918	23/07/1918
Miscellaneous	120th Infy. Bde. 120/443.	31/07/1918	31/07/1918
Miscellaneous	120 Inf Bde.	01/08/1918	01/08/1918
Heading	40th Div. 120th Bde. War Diary 11th Battn. Cameron Hldrs. August 1918.		
War Diary	Sercus.	01/08/1918	11/08/1918
War Diary	Swartenbrouch	12/08/1918	12/08/1918
War Diary	Vieux Berquin.	13/08/1918	31/08/1918
War Diary		27/08/1918	31/08/1918
Heading	40th Div. 120th Bde. War Diary 11th Battn. Cameron Hldrs. September 1918.		
War Diary	Wallon Capell	01/09/1918	11/09/1918
War Diary	Steenwerck.	12/09/1918	13/09/1918
War Diary	In The Field.	14/09/1918	30/09/1918
Miscellaneous	40th Division. No. C/18/A.	08/09/1918	08/09/1918
Heading	40th Div. 120th Bde. War Diary 11th Battn. Cameron Hldrs. October 1918.		
War Diary	Steenwerck.	01/10/1918	02/10/1918
War Diary	Erquinghem.	03/10/1918	05/10/1918
War Diary	Armentieres.	05/10/1918	18/10/1918
War Diary	St Andre.	19/10/1918	28/10/1918
War Diary	Lannoy.	29/10/1918	31/10/1918
Miscellaneous	120th Bde. No. 120/406.	11/10/1918	11/10/1918
Heading	40th Div. 120th Bde. War Diary 11th Battn. Cameron Hldrs. November 1918.		

War Diary	Lannoy	01/11/1918	06/11/1918
War Diary	Estaimpuis.	07/11/1918	09/11/1918
War Diary	Warcoing.	10/11/1918	12/11/1918
War Diary	Nechin.	13/11/1918	30/11/1918
Heading	40th Div. 120th Bde. War Diary 11th Battn. Cameron Hldrs. December 1918.		
War Diary	Nechin.	01/12/1918	19/12/1918
War Diary	Lannoy.	20/12/1918	31/12/1918
Miscellaneous	XV Corps No. I.G. 98/35. dated 21-12-18.	21/12/1918	21/12/1918
Miscellaneous	Headquarters. 120. Infantry Brigade.	25/12/1918	25/12/1918
Heading	40th Div. 120th Bde. War Diary 11th Battn. Cameron Hldrs. January 1919.		
War Diary	Lannoy.	01/01/1919	31/01/1919
Miscellaneous	Not To Be Communicated To The Press.	08/01/1919	08/01/1919
Miscellaneous	To-O.C., 11th Battn Cameron Highlanders Regiment. Through Ed. Qrs 120th Infantry Brigade.	11/01/1919	11/01/1919
Miscellaneous	Army Pay Office A.P.O. S38 B.L.E.	22/01/1919	22/01/1919
Miscellaneous	Army Coy Office, A.P.O. S38 B.L.E.	22/01/1919	22/01/1919
Miscellaneous	Command Paymaster "B" Branch A.P.O. S 38 B.E.F.	21/01/1919	21/01/1919
Miscellaneous	In reply please quote OCE 3/1217 OVN 2297-9.	10/03/1919	10/03/1919
Miscellaneous	To/O.C. "A" Coy. "B" Coy.	26/01/1919	26/01/1919
Miscellaneous	War Office, Whitehall, S.W.	07/01/1919	07/01/1919
Heading	40th Div. 120th Bde. War Diary 11th Battn. Cameron Hldrs. February 1919.		
War Diary	Lannoy.	01/02/1919	28/02/1919
Miscellaneous	A. Gs. No. AG/2158/9113 (O) 40th Division No. 23 (A) 120th Inf. Bde. No. 120/400.	05/02/1919	05/02/1919
Heading	40th Div. 120th Bde. War Diary 11th Battn. Cameron Hldrs. May 1919.		
War Diary	Croix.	01/05/1919	01/05/1919

DO 95/2611/2

40TH DIVISION
120TH INFY. BDE

11TH BN CAMERON HIGH'DRS

JUN 1918-MAY 1919

Formed 1918 JUNE

40th Div.
120th Bde.

WAR DIARY

11th BATTN CAMERON HLDRS.

JUNE
1918

Army Form C. 2118.

WAR DIARY
or
INTELLIGENCE SUMMARY.
(Erase heading not required.)

JUNE 1918
VOLUME I
11th Garr Bn. Cameron Highrs
Vol I

Place	Date	Hour	Summary of Events and Information	Remarks and references to Appendices
Etaples	9/6/18		Lt. Col. O.H. Vivian, M.V.O., D.S.O. took over 130 H.Q. details from the Garr. Bn. Base Depot along with following officers: Major J.S. Gracie, 2nd in Command; Capt. & Adj. J. Neilson; Lieut. J.S. Bruce, Asst. Adj.; Lt. & Q.M. G. Lewington; 2nd Lt. J.S. Gordon, L.G. officer; 2nd Lt. H. Taylor, Bomb. officer; 2nd Lt. L.W.D.R. Williams, Transport officer.	In
do.	10/6/18		H.Q. moves to Le Cinq Rues near Lozinghem in the Watten area and were accommodated in Billets and a few tents.	In
Le Cinq Rues	11/6/18	10 a.m.	The following officers and four Companies arrived - strength 451 O.R. A. Coy. Capt. A. Clermont; Lieut. C. Lebon; 2nd Lt. J.S. Norman; B. Coy Lieut. W.L. Morris; Lieut. R. Craven; C. Coy Captain A.E.S. Curtis, 2nd Lt. J.L. Megan; 2nd Lt. A.H. Kyson; D. Coy Captain R.O. Lunny; Lieut. K.K. Day; Lieut. R.W. Scott; 2nd Lt. B.S. Potts. The men were in Category B1 and they were drawn from 29 different Labour Companies. The next two days were spent in settling down and training commenced on the 14th inst.	In
	14/6/18			In
	15/6/18		C.O. & Coy Offrs. L.G. officer & Intelligence officer proceeded in a lorry to inspect	In

Army Form C. 2118.

WAR DIARY
or
INTELLIGENCE SUMMARY.
(Erase heading not required.)

JUNE 1918
VOLUME I
11
11th Reserve Bn. Cameron Highrs

Place	Date	Hour	Summary of Events and Information	Remarks and references to Appendices
Leaving Area	16/6/18		W. Hazebrouck line 120th Bn. Sector. Lieut. K.R. Young, 2nd Lt. J.W. Russell, 1 W.O. and 8 Sgts. arrive	
	18/6/18		Four Coy officers and 8 NCOs inspected trenches W. Hazebrouck line	In
	20/6/18		D.A.G. G.H.Q. inspected the Bn. with Major General Ponsonby.	In
La Belle Hotines	23/6/18		The Bn. moved to Blaringhem area in a convoy of buses. Accommodation was found for this unit in two fields situated C.14.c.8.6. Sheet 36A N.W.	In
	24/6/18		The officers in tents and the men in bivouacs. The 24th was spent in settling down, and training commenced on the 25th. A rifle range was chosen at the disposal of the Bn. every three mornings and full use was made of it by Coys and Lewis Gunners. The I.S.M. inspected unfit men and reclassified 38 in a lower category. They were sent to Labour Corps Base Depot on 27th June	In
	26/6/18		A trial manning of the trenches to be held was carried out.	In
	27/6/18		The trenches were again manned and posts marked with pegs. After the Bn. took up its position the four Labour Companies to be attached to this unit took up their positions in rear of the line on a support. In	

WAR DIARY
or
INTELLIGENCE SUMMARY.
(Erase heading not required.)

Army Form C. 2118.

JUNE 1918.

VOLUME I

11th Garrn Bn. Cameron Highrs

Place	Date	Hour	Summary of Events and Information	Remarks and references to Appendices
La Belle Hotesse	29/6/18		The G.O.C. 40th Divn decided to transfer Scotchmen to this unit and to Clothing Bn. arrived 251. In exchange 221 Englishmen & Irishmen were sent to units:- 119th, 120th & 121st Bns. The following officers arrived with men:- Capt R.M. Parlie, 2nd Lt J. Booth, & 2nd Lt J. Rutherford. The following officers reported from 121st Bn:- 2nd Lt W.D. Winchester, 2nd Lt W. Hamilton R.N.I. In exchange for these officers the following officers of this unit were transferred to 121st Bn: Captain A. Clermont, Lieut. K.H. King, 2nd Lieut G.S. Potter, J.J. Norman, R.D.W.R. Williams, R. Pease, J.J. Coulin.	
	30/6/18		The following officers of the Black Watch reported from Base:- Lieuts D.J. Guthrie, J. Coutts, W. Dickson, W.H. Pilcher, J. Kinloch, J. Borella - Third, 2nd Lieuts J.E. Scatchard, G.R. Hunter, J.J. Purdie, E.G. Hunter. The weather during the month was fine. An epidemic of Influenza broke out during the month.	

Otho Vivian
Lt. Colonel
Commanding, 11th Garrn Bn. Cameron Highrs.

40th Div. No. 27/4/G.   SECRET.

HEADQUARTERS, 120TH INFANTRY BRIGADE.
No. 120/408
Date...........

S.21

The following General Staff Notes were made at the Conference held at Divisional Headquarters at 11.0 a.m. 21/6/18 :-

1. That Battalion Commanders should explain to the men under their command, the role which the Division has been called upon to fill, and that the enrolment of Class B men in fighting units is necessitated by the shortage of man-power.

2. That instruction should be given to all ranks, by means of lectures.
   Brigade Commanders will furnish a return by 6 p.m. 24th instant, giving the names of officers able to deliver lectures and the subjects upon which they desire to lecture.

3. That training in marching should be progressive, commencing at about 2 miles and gradually increasing the distance to 6 miles.
   On all such parades, a small rear guard will follow the Battalion to ensure that all men who fall out are collected and brought in, in a formed body.

   Straggling is not to be permitted.

4. Battalion Commanders were told to apply for any officers and instructors they require.

5. That application be made for recreational kit and that Recreational training be developed to the fullest possible extent.

                                W Carter
                                Major,
22/6/18.   General Staff, 40th Division.

                                *****

Issued down to Battalions.

OC 11th Edn. Cam. Hrs.

Forwarded for necessary action;
Return called for in para 2 to be rendered
to this office not later than 1 PM 23rd inst.

                                H.B. Kerr
                                CAPTAIN,
                                BRIGADE MAJOR,
                                120th INFANTRY BRIGADE.

22/6/18.

120th Infy Bde.

Reference your 120/408 the following is a list of officers able to give lectures.

Musketry   Capt A.E.S. CURTIS
   do   Capt R.O. LUNN
   do   2nd Lt A.H. LYON

Map reading 2nd Lt J.W. Russell

                              Lt Col
                    11th Gurkha Comm Regt

22/6/18.
Col Nivison can lecture on Organization of Battn, Duties of Officers and Drill book
Major J.T. Brodie can lecture on Interior Economy.

O.C.
A B C D Coy

Please pass
quickly as return
must be rendered
to Bde tonight

J Neilson
Col ?a?

11 Cameron
22/6/18

A Coy
B
C
D

Refer para 2.

This refers to officers who are competent to lecture to NCOs & men in B[attalio]ns on subjects they may have specially studied —

e.g. Map Reading, Musketry, Organization, Field Tactics &c.

Officers able to lecture will please write their names below & state their subject.

Map reading — J M Purnell
Musketry — A H Lyons 2/Lt

[signatures illegible]

40th Div.
120th Bde.

WAR DIARY

11th BATTN. CAMERON H.LDRS.

JULY

1918

JULY 1918.

VOLUME II

WAR DIARY
or
INTELLIGENCE SUMMARY. 11th Garr. Br. Cameron Highlanders

Army Form C. 2118.

Page 1.

(Erase heading not required.)

Place	Date	Hour	Summary of Events and Information	Remarks and references to Appendices
La Belle Hotesse	1/7/18		The Companies were at the disposal of the Company Officers for duty. The Rev. Albert Storr C.F. left reported for duty.	In
	2/7/18		The Bn. was inspected by H.R.H. The Duke of Connaught, K.G. H.T. &. On the conclusion of his inspection H.R.H. expresses great satisfaction at the appearance of the Bn. Major-General J. Ponsonby in handing over the command of the Division to Major-General Sir W.E. Peyton, expresses his appreciation of the loyal co-operation of all ranks and wishes them the best of good luck.	In
	3/7/18		The C.O. inspects the Battn. and thereafter the training programme was carried out. In the afternoon the C.O. and all officers who recently joined the Bn. visited the Br. rector of St. Martin, rev. Maybre week him.	
	4/7/18		Lieut. L. Anderson, 4th Gordons reports for duty. The training programme was interrupted. Companies repairing Rifle Range. 50 O.R. reports from Garr. Battn. Base Depot, and a Coy. Tailor from 2nd Royal Irish Regt.	In
	5/7/18		The training programme was continued	In

WAR DIARY
INTELLIGENCE SUMMARY.
11th Garr. Bn. Cameron Highlanders

JULY 1918. VOLUME II. Page 2.

Army Form C. 2118.

Place	Date	Hour	Summary of Events and Information	Remarks and references to Appendices
La Belle Hôtesse	6/7/18		Companies bathed at Le Romarin and first half of Muckty bowed at La Belle Hôtesse Range. In the evening a very successful concert was held. A platform was erected on the parade ground and a piano was borrowed from another unit. The Brigadier attended.	⎬
	7/7/18		The Batt. commenced a four days tour of duty in the W. Hazebrouck line. Three officers and six NCOs of 31st Div. were attached to assist in the instruction in trench duties. The drought continues.	⎬
	8/7/18		Lieut. W. Bower transferred to 10th K.O.S.B. A. & B. Coys under instruction in trench duties. C. & D. Companies near C.R.E. improving E. Hazebrouck line.	⎬
	9/7/18		C. & D. Companies continued work in E. Hazebrouck line. A. & B. Coys practised trench duties and carried out an interesting Company relief. About 8.30 pm a very heavy thunderstorm commenced but we only got the North edge of it. The day was extremely close. "D" Coy began football. B Coy played a cricket match against 304 Road Construction Coy R.E.	⎬
	10/7/18		Trench duties continued. The Labour Companies attacks has a	⎬

WAR DIARY
or
INTELLIGENCE SUMMARY. 11th A.G. arra Bn.h. aneron ..ight.

Army Form C. 2118.

JULY 1918
VOLUME II
Page 3.

Place	Date	Hour	Summary of Events and Information	Remarks and references to Appendices
La Belle Hotesse	11/7/18		Trial manning of the trenches.	In.
	12/7/18		The Battalion returned to camp. There were several heavy thunder showers. Company baths and were on depare of Company Commanders. Heavy thunder showers all day.	In.
	13/7/18		The Bn. was inspected by Major-General Sir W.P. Peyton KCB. & Commander 40th Division.	In.
	14/7/18		Three cases were tried by F.G.C.M. two were dismissed.	In.
	15/7/18		Promulgation of F.G.C.M. During the night there was an exceptional thunder storm, tents and lines being flooded. Lieut. J.T. Bruce vacated appointment of Scout Off. and Lieut. J. Bonella this was appointed in his place.	In.
	16/7/18		The designation "Garrison" is eliminated from the title of the Bn. L.G. & C.O. Companies fired on Range.	In.
	17/7/18		The 40th Division Concert Party "The Gamecocks" gave a concert to the unit.	In.
	18/7/18		The Band of the 40th Division performed in the evening.	In.
Serques	19/7/18		The Battn. moves to C.3 Central.	In.

WAR DIARY
or
INTELLIGENCE SUMMARY.

JULY 1918
VOLUME II
Part 4. 11th Bn. Cameron Highlanders
Army Form C. 2118.

(Erase heading not required.)

Place	Date	Hour	Summary of Events and Information	Remarks and references to Appendices
Lecive	20/7/18		The C.O. & Company Officers proceeded to inspect W. Haybrouck Area.	
	21/7/18		A Divisional C.of E. parade was held. The Deputy Assistant Chaplain General preached.	
	22/7/18		The Bn. commenced advanced training.	
	23/7/18		Owing to heavy rain the training programme was interrupted.	
	24/7/18		The Bn. has a route march to the trenches and back. While there the companies made themselves familiar with this sector of the line.	
	25/7/18		The training programme was interrupted, 200 men being detailed to complete rifle range.	
	26 and 27/7/18		Heavy rain.	
	28/7/18		Usual events for men. Baths.	
	29/7/18		A Coy on Rifle Range.	
	30/7/18		The Divisional Commander inspects the Bn. at work.	
	31/7/18		Training programme continued.	

Odo Vivian Lt. Col.
Comdg 11th Cameron Highlanders

SECRET.   40th Div. No. 44/6 (G).

"B.A.B. TRENCH CODE NO.4."

O.C. ~~17th Cam H~~

5 ~~Copies~~
~~Copy~~ of "B.A.B Trench Code No. 4" serial No. 9543-
9544-9546-9556-9567............ forwarded herewith.
Please acknowledge receipt on form below :-

  Distribution :-

    Infantry Bde. H.Q., ... 1.
    Bn. H.Q., ... 1.
    Infantry Company. .... 1.
    Pioneer Battalion. .... 1.
    L.T.M. Battery. .... 1.
    Field Company. .... 1.
    C.R.E. .... 1.
    Signal Company. .... 1.
    "A & Q" .... 1.

Officers who hitherto have had no experience of this Code should be practised in its use.

The correction at present in use is :-

"Add 2 to each Group".
"Key letter for correction 'H'."

P.T.O

              Lieut-Colonel,
              General Staff, 40th Division.

7-7-18.

9543 Lieut Bruce. J. T. Bruce Lt.

A2

The Adjt
11th Garr Btl, Cameron Hlds

Ref attached, I accidently put my name on the back for which I have now signed & gave the copy I signed for to Lt. Morrie. However this is in order now.

J.T. Bruce Lt,
Asst Adjt

10/7/18. 9:35 AM

Received from Asst. Adjt. copy of
"B.A.B." no 9546.

9/7/18

Received from Asst. Adjt. copy
of "B.A.B." no 9545

9/7/18

Received from Asst. Adjt one copy
of "B.A.B." no 9544

9/7/18 R. M. Churchill
        O.C. 14 Coy

Received from Asst. Adjt. one
copy of "B.A.B." No 9043.

9/8/17   W. Wilson
                          O.C. First
                          "B" Company

Received one copy of "B.A.B."
No 9567.

                          J.L. Bruce Lt.
9/8/17   Asst. Adjt.

120th Infantry Brigade.

Your Order No 204 Copy dated 8th inst. has been received

J Neilson
Capt & Adjt.
for Lt. Col.
Comdg. 11th Garr. Bn. Cameron High.

9/7/18.

11TH
GARRISON BATTALION,
CAMERON HIGHLANDERS.
No. S. 45
Date. 9/7/18

S 53
R R

HEADQUARTERS,
120TH
INFANTRY BRIGADE.
No. 120/400
Date 15/7/18

To – O.C., 11th Battn: Cameron Highlanders. Regiment

Through Hd.Qrs. 120th Infantry Brigade.

With reference to your recommendations for promotion of Officers, dated 23rd June, 1918.

Authority is given for Capt. A.E.S. CURTIS to wear the badges of MAJOR under C.D.S. 384, Section II (1), pending the approval of G.H.Q.

Attention is directed to the following extract from C.D.S. 384 :-

"As soon as an Officer relinquishes his acting rank owing to his vacating his appointment, the fact will be notified by Commanding Officers direct to the Military Secretary at General Headquarters. The date and reason for relinquishing the rank should be stated."

H.Q., 40th Division.
14th July 1918.
FH.

[Signature]
Major,
D.A.A.G., 40th Division.

15/7/18
Forwarded
11thCm.chrs with
A/Maj/Captain
120th Bde.

120th Infy. Bde. No. 120/443.

S.80.

10th K.O.S.B.
15th K.O.Y.L.I.
14th Cam. Highrs.
No.3 Coy., 40th Div. Train.
Brigade Transport Officer (Capt. TRITTON).

The transport of battalions will for the purpose of Active Operations be divided into two Echelons.

1. Echelon "B".
    Baggage wagons (2nd Line Transport).
    Officers Mess Cart.
    Field Kitchens (when issued).

2. Echelon "A".
    Remainder of 1st Line transport.

Cases may occur when it is desirable to have Echelon "B" further in the rear, in which case orders will be issued from Brigade or Divisional Headquarters for Echelon "B" to come under command of O.C., No. 3 Coy., 40th Divisional Train.

The Brigade Transport Officer will then remain in charge of Echelon "A".

23.7.1918.

H.B.Kerr
Captain,
Staff Captain,
120th Infantry Brigade.

120th Infy. Bde. 120/443.

10th K.O.S.B.
15th K.O.Y.L.I.
11th Cam. Highrs.

With reference to this office No. as above dated 23rd July, 1918, please forward your suggestions - by 1st D.R. 2nd August - as to what Battalion Transport you consider should compose 'A' and 'B' Echelons.

31.7.1918.

2nd Lieut.,
A/Staff Captain,
120th Infantry Brigade.

C24

120 Inf Bde

Ref. 120/443 of 31-7-18 + of 13-7-18

The formation of 1st Line Tspt in Echelons A + B depends on the situation.

In event of operations becoming open warfare conditions the 4 Kitchens, Officers Mess Cart + the 2 water carts should form Echelon B of the 1st Line Tspt. The remainder of the 1st Line Tspt and all pack animals would remain as Echelon A.

The supply of water in this area would be a difficulty. The 4 Coy. L Gun Limbers would have to be used to fetch water in patrol tins.

The question of the transport of the L Gun mobile reserve Am^ntes + the 4 extra A.A. L.Guns requires to be settled.

In the event of active operations taking the form of holding a line the Kitchens + Water Carts should not be sent away with Echelon B.

Odo Vivian
Lt Col
11th Cameron High^rs

1 Aug 18.

40th Div.
120th Bde.

WAR DIARY

11th BATTN. CAMERON HLDRS.

AUGUST
1918

Army Form C. 2118.

WAR DIARY
or
INTELLIGENCE SUMMARY.
(Erase heading not required.)

VOLUME III
AUGUST 1918.
11th Cameron Highlanders

Vol 3

Place	Date	Hour	Summary of Events and Information	Remarks and references to Appendices
Lecca	1/8/18		Training continued. L.G. learners on Range.	In.
	2/8/18		100 men on fatigue completing Le Neuf Iron Range, remainder Bn. Route mch.	In.
	3/8/18		200 men on fatigue at La Belle Hoteese Rifle Range, remainder Bn. Drill and Bath.	In
	4/8/18		Major Grace and 23 other ranks attended an inter-denominational Parade Service held by the Second Army. In the evening the Pipe Band of the 5th Cameron Highlanders performed on the Canada ground.	In.
	5/8/18		Training continued, Lewis Gunners and one Company on it. Range	In.
"	6/8/18		do. do. Bombers throwing lincbomb	In.
	7/8/18		do. do. do.	In.
	8/8/18		do. " do.	In.
			General Sir Herbert L.O. Plumer, G.C.B. & Commanding Second Army inspected the Bn. at work	In.
	9/8/18		Training continued, one Company on Range.	In.
	10/8/18		Training continued	In.

Army Form C. 2118.

VOLUMN III

WAR DIARY
or
INTELLIGENCE SUMMARY.
(Erase heading not required.)

AUGUST 1918.

11th Cameron Highlanders

Place	Date	Hour	Summary of Events and Information	Remarks and references to Appendices
Locon	11/8/18		Major Grace and 23 other ranks attended an inter-denominational Parade Service. At the conclusion of the service they were reviewed by H.M. The King.	In.
Swarten trench	12/8/18		The 120th Infantry Bn. relieved the 121st Infantry Bn. on the sector WEST of VIEUX BERQUIN. This unit relieved the 23rd Cheshire Regt. in the support line.	In
Vieux Berquin	13/8/18		The Battn. moved to the right-section, and relieved the 15th KOYLI and one company of 11th E. Yorks. in support. The front company was shelled rather heavily from M.G. fire (wounded) on casualty.	In.
	14/8/18		Quiet day, the Bn. being employed on working parties after 8 p.m.	do
	15/8/18		Quiet day, working parties at night, two gas alarms during night.	do
	16/8/18		do two S.O.S. signals during night	do
	17/8/18		The Bn. relieved the 15th KOYLI in the line, the 10th KOSB coming into support line. In the early morning Lt. G.S. Young and four men were gassed and two men wounded.	
	18/8/18		B. Coy was troubled throughout day with whizz-bangs. The Bn. front	

WAR DIARY
or
INTELLIGENCE SUMMARY.
(Erase heading not required.)

11th Cameron Highlanders

VOLUMN III
AUGUST 1918   Army Form C. 2118.

Instructions regarding War Diaries and Intelligence Summaries are contained in F. S. Regs., Part II. and the Staff Manual respectively. Title pages will be prepared in manuscript.

Place	Date	Hour	Summary of Events and Information	Remarks and references to Appendices
Vieux Berquin	18/8/18		was constantly shelled throughout the day	In
	19/8/18		Patrols reported enemy line very lightly held. No scratches scouts on patrol encountered a Boch who refused to surrender and was shot by S/Scatcher	In
	20/8/18		Enemy patrols were seen on our front. In the evening A & B. Companies advanced their lines about 800 yards. D. Company relieved B Coy of 10th to Yorks. Regt. on right.	In
	21/8/18		To conform with troops on right and left A & D Companies further advanced their lines and in the evening C Coy came into the line and took over B Coy frontage and half of A, D Company extending to the left to take over the remaining half of A Coy frontage.	
	22/8/18		In the early morning C Company advanced and reached their final objective. At 8.30 p.m. D Company pivoted on their left flank and came in line with unit on right. During the night the Battn was relieved our frontage being	In

WAR DIARY or INTELLIGENCE SUMMARY.
(Erase heading not required.)

VOLUME III
AUGUST 1918
1¹/1 Cameron Highlanders

Army Form C. 2118.

Place	Date	Hour	Summary of Events and Information	Remarks and references to Appendices
Vieux Berquin	22/8/18		occupied by 1st 10th K.O.S.B. and 15th H.L.I. The Bn moved back into 15th H.L.I. position in Reserve. The weather was good during the four days the Bn. was in the front line. During the same period 12 O.R. were killed 2 died of wounds 2 officers and 30 O.R. gassed and 13 sick. The Bn rested in the morning and supplies working parties during night	
	23/8/18		do	
	24/8/18		do	
	25/8/18		do	
	26/8/18		do	
	27/8/18		do	
	28/8/18		Orders received to relieve 15th H.L.I. in the line. Relief complete by 5 am. Battalion somewhat and suffered numerous little casualties difft.	
	29/8/18		opposition	
	30/8/18		Battalion relieved by 25th Lancers. Relief complete by 4.30 am afterwards moved back to Reserve Area and	
	31/8/18		moved into camp near Walton Cappell	

Lt. Col. Grough
1/1 Cameron Highlanders

VOLUME III
AUGUST 1918   Army Form C. 2118.
11th Cameron Highlanders

WAR DIARY
or
INTELLIGENCE SUMMARY.
(Erase heading not required.)

Place	Date	Hour	Summary of Events and Information	Remarks and references to Appendices
	31/8/18 cont.		Burital casualties during the 18 days amounted to:- 14 Killed, 4 Died of wounds, 33 wounded M.G fire and shell fire, 33 wounded gas, 2 S.W., 1 N.Y.D.N. (As no report from F.A received yet as to nature of casualty.) Otto Vincent Lt Col 11th Cameron Highrs	

VOLUME III
AUGUST 1918
Army Form C. 2118.

11th Cameron Highlanders

WAR DIARY
or
INTELLIGENCE SUMMARY.
(Erase heading not required.)

Place	Date	Hour	Summary of Events and Information	Remarks and references to Appendices
	27/8/18.		C & D Companies moved from the 'Z' line to the front-line, & relieved two companies of the K.O.Y.L.I. in the front line. C Company, Bishops Corner and into right of Denver.	
	29/8/18.		A & B Companies moved up in the night and relieved the remaining two companies of the K.O.Y.L.I. in the forward area. The whole wood then over by the Camerons from the K.O.Y.L.I. Relief complete 5 a.m. 29th. At 7.30 p.m. the Battalion advanced under an artillery barrage to the June Bishops Corner – Rue Provost – Bowery Cot., thence S. towards Neuve Berquin, where they were reinforced with the 183 Brigade. In the advance from Bishops Corner to Rue Provost Coy. had several casualties from the hostile barrage. During the night of the 29th the 4/5 Gloster took over the sector relieving our companies who got down about 6 a.m. 30th.	
	30/8/18.		The Battalion rested in the 2 line and Reserve Trenches till 3 p.m. when it marched back to camp near Walton Cappell.	
	31/8/18		In camp near Walton Cappell.	

Otto Vivian
Lt Col.
11 Cameron Highlanders

40th Div.
120th Bde.

WAR DIARY

11th BATTN. CAMERON HLDRS.

SEPTEMBER
1918

WAR DIARY or INTELLIGENCE SUMMARY

September 1918. Volume 1. Army Form C. 2118.

11th Bn Cameron Highlanders

Vol 4

Place	Date	Hour	Summary of Events and Information	Remarks and references to Appendices
WALLON-CAPPEL	1/9/18		Battalion engaged cleaning up. Church services held	App 1
	2/9/18		R.C.s went to Cassel. Bn. Gas NCO's Gas Drill	App 1
	3/9/18		Practice Parade for Divisional General Inspection. Training carried out	App 1
	4/9/18		Inspection by G.O.C. 10 Division. Temp. for training afternoon. Running fixtures carried out	App 1
	5/9/18		Bn. Outpost - Advance Guard Scheme carried out (app 1518) Hy Gunners covered	App 1
	6/9/18		do	App 1
	7/9/18		Brigade Sports held to-day. Bn finally well represented.	App 1
	8/9/18		Church services	App 1
	9/9/18		Outpost Scheme manoeuvres carried out to act wholly later in day	App 1
			specialist training carried out. Remainder - route march	App 1
	10/9/18		A. Hdqrs. employed cleaning up and billets for industry	App 1
	11/9/18		Remainder of Bn. at Baths and specialist training - P.T. and Rifle Exercises	App 1
	12/9/18		Bn. moved to STEENWERCK	App 1
STEENWERCK	13/9/18		Bn moved up to PONT NIEPPE - JESUS FARM Sector. Bn. in support. Relief	App 1
			Completed 9.25 p.m. Relieved 13th E. LANCS	

WAR DIARY
or
INTELLIGENCE SUMMARY

(Erase heading not required.)

Army Form C. 2118.

September 1918.
Volume 1
11th Bn. 10 Cameron Highlanders

Place	Date	Hour	Summary of Events and Information	Remarks and references to Appendices
[ ]	14/9/18		Spasmodic shelling of Battalion area with slight gas shelling	AAA
	15/9/18		A quiet day	AAA
	16/9/18		Bn. Headquarters came in for some shelling - mainly due to an enemy battery which "B" moved up to a front position and released 15 Rds.	AAA
			10th KOSB coming into reserve. Relief complete 11.25 pm	AAA
	17/9/18		Enemy has had habit of S of W shelling this area. Done heavy stuff also. Strafed around B. 8 Hd. Operations	AAA
	18/9/18		Fairly quiet day. 211 T. R. W. M reported moving. Runner also moving. They were going round posts during morning and did not return.	M
	19/9/18		A. Headquarters were subjected to heavy gas shelling during the night. Had to put his posts in relief to KOH. Relief complete 12.50 am. 20 A. Bn.	M
	20/9/18		Bn. commenced wiring front line posts and improved MGS About 9 pm enemy strafed Bn. HQ with HV guns. Head quarters had to clear. New Head quarters established	M
	21/9/18		A fairly quiet day. Our guns harassing enemy during day	M

WAR DIARY
or
INTELLIGENCE SUMMARY.
(Erase heading not required.)

September 1918. Volume 1 Army Form C. 2118.

11th Bn Cameron High[rs]

Place	Date	Hour	Summary of Events and Information	Remarks and references to Appendices
A.U./J/13	22/9/18		Artillery fairly active in retaliation. Support. Hdqrs. struck with pit. agreeshots — short time — due to enemy moving up into positions nearby.	
	23/9/18		Bn. relieved by 23rd Cheshires. Good relief. Coy. post by 11.35 pm. Batt" moved back to Trounced Ave. Bryats & sufficient blankets & cleaned up.	M? M?
	24/9/18		B.W. commenced training.	M?
	25/9/18		Training continued.	M?
	26/9/18		Do — Lewis Gunners on Ranges. One Company at Baths.	M?
	27/9/18		Do Companies at Baths. Worked tactical scheme.	M?
	28/9/18		Training interrupted owing to heavy rain.	In
	29/9/18		Church Service	In
	30/9/18		Training interrupted owing to heavy rain.	L

Otto Vivian
Lt. Col.
Commdg 11th Cameron Highlanders.

CONFIDENTIAL.　　　　　　　　　　　　　40th Division. No. C/18/A.

Headquarters, 120th Inf. Bde.
===================

1. The Divisional Commander wishes it to be impressed upon the Commanders of all Formations and Units that recommendations for Immediate award must be forwarded to Divisional Hd. Qrs. as early as possible after the act has been performed.

2. If recommendations are to receive the consideration due to them they must be forwarded with the least possible delay. In future in cases where delay has occurred a brief statement of the circumstances causing the delay will be forwarded with the recommendations for the information of the Divisional Commander.

3. The originals of recommendations have now to be forwarded to higher authority by these Headquarters, therefore, care must be taken that originals are correctly and carefully made out and written on Army Form W.3121.

　　　　　　　　　　　　　　　　　(Sgd) A. L. COWTAN, Major,
3rd September, 1918.　　　　　　　D.A.A.G., 40th Division.

120th Inf. Bde. No. 120/420.　　　　　　　　　　　　CONFIDENTIAL.

10th Bn. K.O.S.B.
15th Bn. K.O.Y.L.I.
11th Bn. Cam. Highrs.
120th T. M. Battery.
===================

1. Recommendations for Immediate awards must be submitted without delay if Unit Commanders wish to get the decorations for the Officers and Other Ranks under their Command.

2. As originals of A.F. W.3121 have to be forwarded to Divisional Headquarters it will not be possible to correct the frequent mistakes which appear at present in the forms when they reach this office. If the recommendations are not complete and correct, delay is bound to occur, as they will have to be returned to be amended.

3. Too much care cannot be taken in the wording of the recommendations. For Immediate awards some <u>definite</u> act of gallantry must be brought to notice. Recommendations for continuous devotion to duty should be withheld for the half yearly honours gazette.
　　The wording should be as concise as possible consistent with clearness and no reference should be made to the length of time the person recommended has been in the country, or to the fact that no previous reward has been given.

- 2 -

4. Full instructions are given in S.S. 477a which should be carefully studied.

5. The following points are emphasized as mistakes in them frequently occur:-

(a) <u>Full</u> christian names <u>before</u> surname.

(b) Substantive rank always to be given, e.g.
2nd Lieut.(T/Captn). or T/Lieut.(A/Captn).
Corporal (L/Sgt). or Pte. (A/Sgt).

(c) When it is known that the name of an Officer is incorrectly stated in the Army List, a note to that effect should be added.

(d) Recommendations for Officers of Substantive rank of Major or lower for the D.S.O. must be supported by the written evidence of an eyewitness.

(e) Any previous decorations awarded must be stated on the form.

(f) The Signature of the C.O. must be dated.

(g) A single copy only of A.F. W.3121 is required, but <u>never</u> be more than <u>one</u> name on each form.

T. Knox-Shaw
Captain,
Staff Captain,
120th Infantry Brigade.

8-9-18.

40th Div.
120th Bde.

WAR DIARY

11th BATTN. CAMERON HLDRS.

OCTOBER
1918

Army Form C. 2118.

WAR DIARY
or
INTELLIGENCE SUMMARY.
(Erase heading not required.)

October 1918.
Volume 1
11th -13th Cameron Highlanders
Vol 5

Place	Date	Hour	Summary of Events and Information	Remarks and references to Appendices
STEENWERCK	1/10/18	2030	The 120th Infantry Bde relieved the 121st Infy Bde on the Right Bde Front. The 11th Camerons relieved the 23rd Lanc. Fusiliers in Reserve	In.
	2/10/18		"D" Coy relieved one Company of the 10th K.O.S.B. at TIG FARM on the Right front line. The K.O.S.B. crossed the Lys. Quiet day and night	In
ERQUINGHEM	3/10/18	1900	The 13th moved to ERQUINGHEM area. B.C. and D Companies in ERQUINGHEM, A.B.'s and A Company north of the LYS.	In
	4/10/18	0500	B Company occupied the ERQUINGHEM SWITCH in support to K.O.S.B. 0800 A.B and D Companies were employed under C.R.E.	In
	5/10/18	0700	A.B and D Companies were employed under C.R.E.	
		1900	The 11th Camerons relieved the 10th K.O.S.B. on the line, B Company on the line, C in support, and A and D Companies in reserve	In
ARMENTIERES	6/10/18	2300	B Coy in the line were relieved by the 15th H.L.I. and withdrew to a position near the Asylum, ARMENTIERES. Quiet day and night.	In

Army Form C. 2118.

WAR DIARY
or
INTELLIGENCE SUMMARY.
(Erase heading not required.)

October 1918
Volume 1
11th Cameron Highlanders

Place	Date	Hour	Summary of Events and Information	Remarks and references to Appendices
ARMENTIERES	7/10/18	1800	A and D Companies moved to position N of ARMENTIERES about C.20 in support, and suy flews on the tactical disposal of the 2/c 15th K.O.Y.L.I. holding the outpost line. Major J.J. Grant took command of the two Companies. They maintained themselves in posts covering the bridge over the LYS.	In.
	9/10/18	2000	The 10th K.O.S.B. relieved the 11th Cameron High. in support.	
		2200	The 11th Cameron Highlanders relieved the 15th K.O.Y.L.I. in the outpost line. D Company on the right. B Company on the centre and C Company on the left. 2/Lieut. R. Company in support. Lieut. R.R. Day A. Transport officer was wounded whilst delivering rations to Bn. H.Q.	In.
	10/10/18	1500	Bn. H.Q. established near HOUPLINE STATION. C Company took line of residence near HOUPLINE STATION. C Company took up quarters near the line of residence in front of HOUPLINE	In.
	11/10/18	1000	D Coy on the right made an attempt to occupy the old enemy front line. This was unsuccessful owing to the B Company	

WAR DIARY or INTELLIGENCE SUMMARY

Army Form C. 2118.

October 1918. Volume 1.
11th Bn Cameron High[landers]

Place	Date	Hour	Summary of Events and Information	Remarks and references to Appendices
ARMENTIERES	11/10/18		made a slight advance to the British old support line	In
	12/10/18	05.15	with the aid of artillery one Company of the 10th K.O.S.B. carried out a minor operation assisting in INCANDESCENT SUPPORT just west of railway and advancing northwards along the support trench and mopping up the FRONT line trench	
		23.00	The Cameron 11th Cameron High[landers] took over the line taken by the K.O.S.B. "B" Coy went back into reserve.	In
	13/10/18	19.00	The 120th Infantry Bde was relieved in the advanced sector (Sector by the 121st Inf Bde, the 11th Cameron High[landers] being relieved by the 8th A.R. Scot. Reg. After relief the Camerons proceeded to Camp at GOSPEL VILLA W of ARMENTIERES BHQ at SKINAFINT FARM During the tour in the line 2 Officers were wounded, Lieut R. Day, and 2nd Lt. A. McTavish (with 231st Field Coy R.E.) 1 O.R. died of wounds, 4 O.R. wounded, 1 O.R. accid[entally] wounded and 12 O.R. wounded (Gas)	In
	14/10/18		Employed about the day cleaning up	

WAR DIARY or INTELLIGENCE SUMMARY

Army Form C. 2118.

OCTOBER 1918 VOLUME I

11th Bn Cameron Highlanders

Place	Date	Hour	Summary of Events and Information	Remarks and references to Appendices
	15/10/18		Battalion employed clearing up. Commanding Officer inspected new Drill and training of Young Soldiers & Bombers commenced	
	16/10/18		Rain interfered with training during morning. Specialists trained indoors. Orders received that enemy going back. Battn moved up to L'ERQUINGHEM.	m.
	17/10/18		Bupto in support.	m.
	18/10/18		Battalion moved forward to LA PREVOTE by road route	m.
	19/10/18		Battalion moved to NAMBRECIES Battalion in Billets here. Inhabitants gave troops a good welcome	m.
ST ANDRE	20/10/18		Battalion moved to ST ANDRE & good billets	m.
	21/10/18		Battalion employed on working parties during morning. Cleaning up and drill during afternoon. Specialist training continued	m.
	22/10/18		Battn having during morning & employed on working parties during afternoon	m.
	23/10/18		Battn continued to supply working parties. 2 Coys morning 2 in afternoon. Training continued. Young Soldiers & Bombers & Scouts officially trained	m.
	24/10/18		Work and training continued. Rifle Range which was enthuces yesterday	m.

OCTOBER 1918
VOLUME V
Army Form C. 2118.

1st Bn Cameron Highlanders

WAR DIARY
or
INTELLIGENCE SUMMARY.
(Erase heading not required.)

Place	Date	Hour	Summary of Events and Information	Remarks and references to Appendices
ST AMORE	24/10/18		was utilised to day for firing	App.
	25/10/18		Training took continued. Firing carried out	App.
	26/10/18		Do	App.
	27/10/18		Battalion employed working on railway during whole day	App.
	28/10/18		Battalion moved by muncle parts to LANNOY. A long march, but men stood it splendidly. Billets Barnes in support	App.
LANNOY	29/10/18		Battalion continued training. Battle formation practised	App.
	29/10/18		and continues. Intensive training of specialists. Two Companies	App.
	30/10/18		at Rifle Range during afternoon	App.
			Training continued	

Geo Gordon
Lt Col
1 Cameron High

S 191

120th Inf. Bde. No. 120/406.   SECRET.

10th Bn. K.O.S.B.
15th Bn. K.O.Y.L.I.
11th Bn. Cam. Highrs.

On night 12/13th instant, the 11th Bn. Cam. Highrs. will relieve the Company of the 10th K.O.S.B. who are carrying out the attack. This Company will move back to its proper position replacing the Company of the 15th Bn. K.O.Y.L.I. which will return to its battalion. Completion of relief will be wired by 11th Cam. Hrs. to Brigade Headquarters using code word :-

"BUNKUM"

Captain,
Brigade Major,
120th Infantry Brigade.

11-10-18.

R.6.

40th Div.
120th Bde.

WAR DIARY

11th BATTN. CAMERON HLDRS.

NOVEMBER

1918

WAR DIARY VOLUME I

NOVEMBER 1918
INTELLIGENCE SUMMARY — 11th Battalion Inniskilling(?) Fusiliers

Army Form C. 2118.

Instructions regarding War Diaries and Intelligence Summaries are contained in F. S. Regs., Part II. and the Staff Manual respectively. Title pages will be prepared in manuscript.

(Erase heading not required.)

Place	Date	Hour	Summary of Events and Information	Remarks and references to Appendices
BAVAY	1-11-18		Enemy carried out particularly active operations	J.M.
	2-11-18		Enemy continued their S. & Retirement being not being met by opposing unit(?)	J.M.
			Range & Tongue Tactical features covered out by Opposing unit(?) Troops	J.M.
	3-11-18		Advance Parties held.	J.M.
	4-11-18		Enemy Tactical weapons carried out with Troops. Passing down to Officers and Running movement	J.M.
	5-11-18		Two long days of hard training for young officers	J.M.
	6-11-18		Battalion moved to Bettencourt arriving near new billets. Goods to Wavrechin reparted(?)	J.M. J.M.
	7-11-18		Rest day. Improved training commenced	J.M.
	8-11-18		Running & voluntary Instruction games on Rifle Exercises and	J.M.
ESTRAMBRIS			Enemy withdrew from the SOLRE r. 119 Inf Bde. crossed in pursuit.	
	9-11-18		Battalion moved by motor lorries to Wavrechin Positions on Belgian clan(?)	J.M.
			Watering and Refit. Intermittent rain of autumn.	J.M.

Army Form C. 2118.

WAR DIARY VOLUME I
NOVEMBER 1918 for
INTELLIGENCE SUMMARY. 11th Cameron Highlanders

(Erase heading not required.)

Instructions regarding War Diaries and Intelligence Summaries are contained in F. S. Regs., Part II. and the Staff Manual respectively. Title pages will be prepared in manuscript.

Place	Date	Hour	Summary of Events and Information	Remarks and references to Appendices
WARGOING	10-11-18	—	Church parade held.	App
	11-11-18	—	Battalion employed on Working Parties. Armistice announced officially reported signing hostilities cease at 11.00 hours	App
	12-11-18	—	Battalion march past to Return at Nechin	App
NECHIN	13-11-18	—	Battalion commenced inspection by C.O. Drill exercises and recreational drill practice	App
	14-11-18	—		App
	15-11-18	—	Brigade continued drill exercises. Gas respirator drill	App
	16-11-18	—	Chiefest work month end other Battalion on march	App
	17-11-18	—	Church parade held. Corps sports held at Roubaix. Services	App
	18-11-18	—	Brigade commander inspected B Coy billets re demobilization	App
	19-11-18	—	Brigade commander inspective ie Corps Commander who commented on the good appearance of the men much pride with service and education attended divine service	App

A6945 Wt. W14422/M160 350,000 12/16 D.D. & L. Forms/C/2118/14.

Army Form C. 2118.

WAR DIARY VOLUME I
INTELLIGENCE SUMMARY. 11th Cameron Highlanders
NOVEMBER 1918

(Erase heading not required.)

Instructions regarding War Diaries and Intelligence Summaries are contained in F. S. Regs., Part II. and the Staff Manual respectively. Title pages will be prepared in manuscript.

Place	Date	Hour	Summary of Events and Information	Remarks and references to Appendices
NECHIN	20-11-18	—	One Coy on Range, rest at Baths. Remainder carry out route march and training.	[A]
	21-11-18		Training carried out.	[A]
	22-11-18		One Company on range. Remainder of Battalion on route march. Bowlers carried out rifle practise.	[A]
	23-11-18		Ceremonial & Company carried out Church service held.	[A]
	24-11-18		Battalion on route march during morning. Battalion Sports held in afternoon. Divisional Band played selections. Sports round very successful.	[A]
	25-11-18		and men attended Commanders dinner.	[A]
	26-11-18		Battalion paraded for inspection of Commanding Officer.	[A]
	27-11-18		Training continued. A Coy inspected by Brigadier.	[A]
	28-11-18		One Coy on range. Remainder of Battalion continue training. Party employed cleaning billets at Lannoy, in preparation for Battalion moving there.	[A]
	29-11-18		Training continued. Battalion Football team played 15th K.O.Y.L.I. while resulted in a draw.	[A]

Army Form C. 2118.

WAR DIARY VOLUME. I
NOVEMBER 1918
INTELLIGENCE SUMMARY. 11th Cameron Highlanders

(Erase heading not required.)

Instructions regarding War Diaries and Intelligence Summaries are contained in F. S. Regs., Part II. and the Staff Manual respectively. Title pages will be prepared in manuscript.

Place	Date	Hour	Summary of Events and Information	Remarks and references to Appendices
NECHIN	30/11/18		One Coy on range. Remainder on Route march.	App 1

Odo Finan
Lt Col
11 Cameron Highlanders

R.7

40th Div.
120th Bde.

WAR DIARY

11th BATTN. CAMERON HLDRS.

DECEMBER
1918

WAR DIARY

of 11th Battn. CAMERON HIGHLANDERS
INTELLIGENCE SUMMARY. DECEMBER 1918

Army Form C. 2118. VOLUME I.

Instructions regarding War Diaries and Intelligence Summaries are contained in F. S. Regs., Part II. and the Staff Manual respectively. Title pages will be prepared in manuscript.

(Erase heading not required.)

Place	Date	Hour	Summary of Events and Information	Remarks and references to Appendices
NECHIN	1st	-	Church service held. Battalion Bathed.	—
	2	-	Battalion training and educational classes continued.	—
	3	-	Training continued. B. Coy inspected by Brigadier.	—
	4	-	Battalion paraded for Divisional inspection. Parade cancelled owing to inclement weather.	—
	5	-	Training continued.	—
	6	-	Ranges allotted to Battalion. Divisional Boxing Tournament commenced. About 150 men marched to Roubaix to witness same.	—
	7	-	Battalion derived out Route march. Coy Kitchens won by Battalion evening Coy Kitchens. Boxing tournament continued. Light night.	—
	8	-	Church service held.	—
	9	-	Training continued. C. Coy inspected by Brigadier. 8 Officers and 40 O.R. proceed by Bus to visit Lille.	—
	10	-	Brazil's Divisional Tournament parade held.	—
	11	-	Battalion training continued.	—
	12	-	Battalion training continued.	—

Army Form C. 2118.

WAR DIARY
VOLUME I
of 1/4th BATH. CAMERON HIGHLANDERS
DECEMBER 1918
INTELLIGENCE SUMMARY.
(Erase heading not required.)

Instructions regarding War Diaries and Intelligence Summaries are contained in F. S. Regs., Part II. and the Staff Manual respectively. Title pages will be prepared in manuscript.

Place	Date	Hour	Summary of Events and Information	Remarks and references to Appendices
NECHIN	13		A, B and C Coys on Ranges. 50. O.R's attended lecture by Chief S.A. Instructor. Remainder on Reorganisation. D Coy inspected by Brigadier General.	
	14		Concert party gave first performance today	A
			Divisional parade for Divisional Inspection but cancelled owing to weather. Later Battalion carried out Route march.	A
	15		Church service held and Baths allowed to Battalion.	A A
	16		Training continued.	A
	17		Divisional ceremonial parade held. Inspection by Corps Commander who accorded very high praise on the appearance and smart rest of the men. Brigade sweepstake for War Bonds drawn today. Battalion drew amongst others 1st prize of £25.	A
	18		Training continued. 2 Coys and Battalion H.Q. move to new billets in Lannoy.	A A
	19		Remaining 2 Coys move to Lannoy. Regimental Mess commenced.	A A
LANNOY	20		Training continued	A
	21		Coy Commanders carry out kit inspection	A

WAR DIARY
or INTELLIGENCE SUMMARY.

of 1/4 Batt. CAMERON HIGHLANDERS

VOLUME I.

DECEMBER 1918

Army Form C. 2118.

(Erase heading not required.)

Place	Date	Hour	Summary of Events and Information	Remarks and references to Appendices
LANNOY	22		Church service held.	
	23		Battalion carried out Route march	
	24		Training continued	
	25		Christmas Day. Church service held.	
	26		Boxing Day. Battalion holiday.	
	27		Training continued	
	28		Coy Commanders carry out slit inspection. C.O. inspects A Coy	
	29		Church service held. Battalion services.	
	30		Training continued. + Officers of D.O.O Ranks proceed by Bus to	
			was Lille	
	31		Training continued	

Odo Vivian
Lt Col
11" Cameron H.

S-09

[Stamp: HEADQUARTERS, INFANTRY BRIGADE]

S E C R E T.

XV Corps No.I.G.98/35.
dated 21-12-18.

XV Corps.

G.H.Q., have authorised the withdrawal of the B.A.B. Trench Code.

Please take the necessary measures for collecting all copies of B.A.B. Trench Code distributed to your units, and return them to this office.

        sd. P.F. DALE, Lieut.
   for Lieut-General, General Staff.

Fifth Army "I"
18th Dec. 1918.

2.

                  40th Div. No. 44/17 (G).

A. & Q.
C.R.A.,
C.R.E.,
Div. Sig. Coy.
119th Inf. Bde.
120th Inf. Bde.
121st Inf. Bde.
17th (P) Worc. Rgt.
39th Bn. M.G.C.
=#=#=#=#=#=#

All copies of the B.A.B. Trench Code should be returned forthwith to Div. H.Q., together with an explanation of any deficiencies.

                [signature] Major,
            General Staff, 40th Division.

22-12-18.

O. C.
11th Bn Cameron Highlanders.

Please return the following copies of the B.A.B. Trench Code No 4 issued to your Bn on the 9/7/18

9543. 9544. 9546. 9551. 9567

An explanation of any deficiencies is required.

At the same time the corrections to the Code issued at various dates should also be returned if still in your possession.

T. Knox Shaw Capt.
Brigade Major 120 Inf Bde.

Headquarters,   SECRET

    120. Infantry Brigade.

With reference to your No 120/470.

Herewith five copies of the B.A.B. Trench Code No 4,

numbered 9543, 9544, 9546, 9551, 9567, and corrections

dated 1/9/18, 17/9/18, and 1/11/18.

Please acknowledge receipt hereon

                            J. Neilson
                              Capt & adj.

25/12/18.   for Lt. Col.

            Commanding 11 Battn Cameron Highlanders.

OC/16 Cameron Highlanders

        Received

             Vivian Shaw Croft
             Bde Major, 120 Inf Bde

25/12/18

R.8

40th Div.
120th Bde.

WAR DIARY

11th BATTN. CAMERON HLDRS.

JANUARY

1 9 1 9.

4° January 1919
1/11th Cameron Highlanders
VOLUME I

WAR DIARY
INTELLIGENCE SUMMARY
(Erase heading not required.)

Army Form C. 2118.

Place	Date	Hour	Summary of Events and Information	Remarks and references to Appendices
LANNOY	Jan 1st		New Year's Day Holiday. Intentions have been made to the new Canteen & Dancing arrangements.	
	2		Battalion Training commenced and must soon to the move now ordered duting.	
	3		Training continued. G.O.C. 120th Inf. Bde. made detailed inspection of Battalion Books and Kit, also organisation for Demobilisation.	
	4		Rapid march carried out. Orders ordered to Battalion and Quarterly Audit of P.R.I. carried out.	
	5		Intimate enquiry held.	
	6		Training continued	
	7		do do	
	8		A.F. Z/16 suggesting arrangements made for all men to complete Training continued.	
	9		do	
	10		to Ordino attended to. Entire division to practise Trooping of Colours.	

WAR DIARY of 1/11th Cameron Highlanders

INTELLIGENCE SUMMARY

Army Form C. 2118.

January 1919. Volume I.

Place	Date	Hour	Summary of Events and Information	Remarks and references to Appendices
Lowestoft	Jan 11th		Parties detailed to practise Trooping of Colours. Inspection of Kits.	MSS
"	12		Church service held.	MSS
"	13		Battalion rehearsal for presentation of colours.	MSS
"	14		Battalion on Range. Parties detailed to practise Trooping of colours.	MSS
"	15		Battalion rehearsal for presentation of colours.	MSS
"	16		Training continued. Parties detailed to practise Trooping of Colours.	MSS
"	17		Battalion practises ceremonial parade for Presentation of Colours.	MSS
"	18		Battalion practised ceremonial parade for presentation of colours.	MSS
"	19		Church services held.	MSS
"	20		Consecration & presentation of colours to the Battalion. Officers invited to dinner in commemoration of this occasion. Appreciation of the Brigadier-General read to all ranks on this excellent display.	MSS

January 1919

WAR DIARY or INTELLIGENCE SUMMARY

Army Form C. 2118.

1/4th Cameron Highlanders

Place	Date	Hour	Summary of Events and Information	Remarks and references to Appendices
Lanrey	Jan 21st 1919		Battalion carried out training	MAD
"	22nd		Lecture on the "War of 1870 and the present War." by Mr Hairfield to Battalion	MAD
"	23rd		Route March carried out. Aboard assembled to Examine Battalion file and destroy unnecessary correspondence	MAD
"	24th		Training carried out. Commanding Officer congratulated Sgt Barin on having received the M.S.M.	MAD
"	25th		Battalion paraded for the Baths. K.K. inspected by C.O. Address by B.Gen Sir B. de Lisle Commdg. XV Corps on the presentation of colours sent to all Ranks	MAD MAD
"	26th		Church Service held.	MAD
"	27th		Battalion Carried out training. All Blankets fumigated.	MAD
"	28th		Battalion carried out training	MAD
"	29th		Battalion carried out training	MAD
"	30th		Battalion carried out training. Men proceeded to their respective Bath	MAD

January 1919

WAR DIARY
of 9th Cameron Highlanders
INTELLIGENCE SUMMARY.

Volume I

Army Form C. 2118.

Place	Date	Hour	Summary of Events and Information	Remarks and references to Appendices
Lanacy	Jany 31st 1919		Battalion carried out swimming Mess parade for weekly Bath & change of clothing. During the month of January 3 Officers and 199 O.R. were demobilised	

J.C. Jones Major
O.C. 11th Batt: Cameron Hylrs

CONFIDENTIAL.

A.G./7337 (O).

S 211

NOT TO BE COMMUNICATED TO THE PRESS.

To all Officers Commanding Units.

I wish to impress on all Commanding Officers the necessity for their taking a personal interest, from motives of patriotism, in the speedy enrolment of men for service in the Army after the War.

I feel very strongly that the safety and prosperity of the Empire during the next few years call urgently for the maintenance of an efficient and loyal permanent force. And I look upon it as the duty of one and all of us to induce as many as possible of the good men, now hesitating as to their future careers, to continue to serve both in the interests of their country and of themselves.

The War Office have been asked to consider the issue of a poster in a readily intelligible form, setting forth the conditions of service, pay, pension, etc.

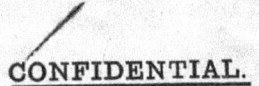

**General Headquarters,
1st Echelon.**
8th January, 1919.

*Commander-in-Chief,
British Armies in France.*

PRINTED IN FRANCE BY ARMY PRINTING AND STATIONERY SERVICES.

PRESS A—1/19.

S 212

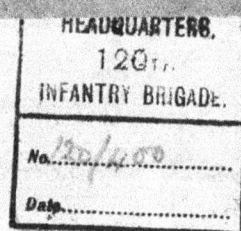
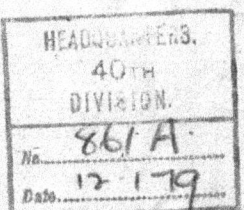

To - O.C., 11th Battn: Cameron Highlanders................ Regiment.

Through Hd. Qrs. 120th .... Infantry Brigade.

With reference to your recommendations for promotion of Officers, dated 5Th January............1919.

Authority is given for 2nd Lieut. J.E. SCATCHERD

to wear the badges of .... CAPTAIN .... under

C.D.S. 384, Section II (1), pending the approval of G. H. Q.

Attention is directed to the following extract from

C.D.S. 384:-

"As soon as an Officer relinquishes his acting rank owing to his vacating his appointment, the fact will be notified by Commanding Officers direct to the Military Secretary at General Headquarters. The date and reason for relinquishing the rank should be stated."

H.Q., 40th Division.
11th January,......1919.
(EH).

A. L. Cowtan.
Major,
D.A.A.G., 40th Division.

Forwarded
H.Q. Camerons
OC 120 Bde

In reply please quote O.Y.N/2297-9
and address to
Command Paymaster,
B. Branch,
A.P.O. S.38, B.E.F.

S 216

Army Pay Office,
A.P.O. S38
B.E.F.
22nd January 1919

DRESSING.

CONFIDENTIAL

(R)

Memorandum for:-

Officer Commanding,
11th Cameron Hldrs, B.E.F. France.

re 2/Lt. A. MacTAVISH of your unit

The above mentioned Officer drew from the Army Ordnance Department on 1/8, 2/8 & 16/10 1918 stores to the value of £10-7-7 and authorised that amount to be recovered from Messrs Holt & Co.

His authority has been returned by them as they do not hold sufficient funds to meet the claims.

Will you kindly cause a remittance to be sent at once, to clear up this charge.

It is proposed to recover by deduction from allowances if the charge is not met within fourteen days from date of this memo.

Capt.
Lieutenant,
for Command Paymaster
British Expeditionary Force.

S 216

In reply please quote
~~Debits~~ OVNJ 2297-9

Army Pay Office,
A.P.O. S38
B.E.F.

22nd January 1919

PRESSING

CONFIDENTIAL

(R)

Memorandum for:-

Officer Commanding,

11th Cameron Hldrs, B.E.F. France.

re 2/Lt. A. MacTAVISH of your unit

The above mentioned Officer drew from the Army Ordnance Department on 1/6, 2/8 & 16/10 1918 stores to the value of £10-7-7 and authorised that amount to be recovered from Messrs Holt & Co.

His authority has been returned by them as they do not hold sufficient funds to meet the claims.

Will you kindly cause a remittance to be sent at once, to clear up this charge.

It is proposed to recover by deduction from allowances if the charge is not met within ~~twenty one~~ fourteen days from date of this memo.

~~Lieutenant~~ Capt.
for Command Paymaster
British Expeditionary Force.

Confidential

Command Paymaster
B. Branch
A.P.O. S 38 BEF

Reference your
O&N/2297-9 d/- 22/1/19.
2/Lt. A MacTavish
proceeded on leave
on 29/12/18 and as he
has not returned
it would appear that he
has been demobilised
It is suggested
that the charge be recovered
from his Gratuity

Major
Comdg 11 Cam H.yf

27/1/19

O.C.,
11th Bn, Cameron Hdrs.,
B. E. F.

<u>Confidential.</u>

In reply please quote
OCE 3/1217 OVN 2297-9

In reply to your letter of the 5th inst., I have to inform you that the charge of £10: 7: 7 in respect of Ordnance Issues obtained by 2/Lieut. A. MacTavish has now been met by his Agents, Messrs. Holt & Co.

Base Pay Office,
France,
10th March, 1919.

Captain,
for Command Paymaster,
"B" Branch.

CONFIDENTIAL.

S217

To/o.C.
"A" Coy. R-M-L-
"B" Coy.

    The attached copy of a letter written by the Adjutant
General, War office to Army Commanders will be read and
thoroughly explained to your men.

    Please pass to the o.C. "B" Coy who will return
to orderly Room after reading to his Company.

                          Neilson
                                Capt: & Adjt:

26-1-19.   11th. Battalion Cameron Highlanders.

War Office,
Whitehall,
S.W.

7th. January 1919.

My dear General,

With reference to the recruiting effort now being made to secure men for the Post-Bellum Army, it is felt that a certain impetus would be given if the subject were presented to the men in a more engaging manner than that which at present obtains. Like all other contracts the bare enumeration of terms in "Leaflet 'A'" makes rather dry reading. It is, of course, necessary to define formally the terms and conditions of service but the supplementation of this by an appeal to the imagination would act as a stimulus.

Most of the men amongst whom we are now recruiting have no experience of service in the Army in peace conditions, and no doubt many picture another four years service as very much like the years which have gone (less the element of danger). Consequently Army life may not seem very attractive. It would dispel this idea if leaflets were widely issued emphasing the brighter side of Army life.

The following headings are suggested:-

Financial.

The soldier will serve on financial conditions more favourable than those which have ever before obtained in the history of the British Army. The poorest paid man will have at least a clear 10/6 to himself per week, and the scale of pay and allowances rises steadily in accordance with rank and number of dependents until in the higher ranks an aggregate of some five pounds per week is drawn by the soldier and his dependents.

The value of a man's wages lies not so much in what he draws weekly as in what is left to him weekly after all expenses are paid. In civil life today prices are so high that not only is there in very many cases practically nothing left of a working-man's wages at the end of the week, but it requires very carefull management to make ends meet. The soldier is freed from this. In food alone he has a great advantage over the civilian, for the soldier's ration is far greater than that purchased by families in civil life, and the quality much better.

The bounty, too, is no small consideration, and even if the soldier is not so minded as to put by savings from his pay he can, without sacrifice, assure himself of £50 at the end of four years.

Notwithstanding this high rate of pay and the bounty men are further favoured by being permitted in certain circumstances to continue on for pension, and in this connection it is pointed out that it would take a very considerable amount of capital to provide the equivalent even of such a small pension as seven shillings per week.

Educational.

In the peacetime army facilities will be afforded for men to qualify themselves for any of a large variety of civil professions.

In most Garrison towns, too, there are Army Schools which the children of the soldiers may attend, and it is generally admitted that these Schools are better than the average public elementary school.

Domestic.

The married establishment now admissible is far in excess of that which formerly obtained in peace. When not in quarters families "on the strenght" are given lodgings allowance in lieu. Medical attendance and comforts are provided, and travelling accomodation by sea and land. When travelling privately on holidays families are eligible to receive railway concessions.

As a large number of the men who ar now re-engage will be required to serve abroad those families who wish to proceed abroad, and for whom no accomodation can be found will be given opportunities for foreign travel which will never occur in civil life. A fair allowance of personal baggage (based on the number in family) is carried free, and to families occupying Government quarters necessary articles of furniture are issued at all military stations. Families who do not wish to proceed abroad, or for whom accomodation cannot be found, will be at liberty to reside wherever they wish in the United Kingdom and will receive separation allowance in lieu of quarters.

In peace time it is not an uncommon feature for men stationed abroad to find good openings in civil life, much better than can be found at Home, and often discharged men voluntarily stay on as civilians where they formerly served as soldiers.

Sport and Recreation.

There is no other institution which affords the working man such fine facilities for recreation and all kinds of sports as the Army in peace time.

Every garrison has its series of football and cricket clubs, etc., and days and half-days are freely granted to all who take part in games. Some stations have also the advantage of sea-side sports - boating, swimming, etc., - and foreign stations present special advantages for hunting, shooting, etc., to take part in which leave is periodically given.

Indoor recreation is also catered for, in messes and other institutions, and dances, concert parties, etc., are regular features.

In civil life the expense of these recreations would be prohibitive if indulged in on a large scale, but this is not so in the Army owing to the help received from various regimental funds.

Furlough.

Furlough is granted as soon as possible to men who engage for further service, and if it chances that any during the period of their re-engagement happen to serve for a while in the United Kingdom, they will be eligible for the annual leave granted during what is known as "the furlough season" to the troops at home. When serving abroad local leave is given for sports, etc., as and when circumstances admit.

The fact that 50% of dispersal drafts are from now onwards to consist of men continuing to serve in the post-bellum army will give the men enlisting an undoubted advantage in obtaining priority to come home. The desire for 2 or 3 months freedom and rest at home on pay and allowances is probably more attractive to many of the men than actual final demobilisation.

Return to Civil Life.

Men who re-engage under the special terms now offered will not be liable to be compulsorily retained in the Service an extra year if it happens that at the end of their engagement they are serving abroad. This obligation was imposed on the old army, but will not apply to men now re-engaging in the above conditions.

In the past a certain number of posts in Government Service have been reserved for ex-soldiers, and endeavours are being made to greatly increase the number of posts so reserved and to improve their grading.

Special training for civil life has already been alluded to, and this includes training for the literary examination which must be passed to qualify for certain pists in the Civil Service. With regard to the latter soldiers are particularly favoured in that, although they may be over the age prescribed for civilian candidates for the Civil Service they are permitted to make certain deductions (equivalent to the amount of service) from their actual age such as will, as a rule, bring them down to within th prescribed limitation.

        Yours sincerely,
          G.C.C.Macdonagh.

R.9

40th Div.
120th Bde.

WAR DIARY

11th BATTN. CAMERON HLDRS.

FEBRUARY
1 9 1 9.

WAR DIARY
INTELLIGENCE SUMMARY

Army Form C. 2118.

Volume I

Vol 1

(Erase heading not required.)

11th Battalion Cameron Highlanders

Place	Date	Hour	Summary of Events and Information	Remarks and references to Appendices
Lanark	1919 Feb 1st		M.O.'s weekly inspection. Commanding Officer inspects kit of Men.	/CWD
	2nd		Church Service held	/CWD
	3rd-10th		Training carried out. Board assembles to audit Sgts Mess books /CWD on the 3rd. Members their weekly Bath on the 5th. A Pilot	/CWD
			Material arrived in room under Sgts Mess on the 6th.	/CWD
			Battalion moved into C.P.D Coys 65 Rgts on the 8th, also M.O.	/CWD
			weekly inspection from 1st Feby to 10th Feby. 4 officers 180 O.R. were demobilized.	/CWD
	11th		M.O. weekly inspection 15th. Church Service held 16th.	/CWD
		11.28	Inspections of Cadre Army of occupation men by Commanding Officer.	/CWD
			Battalion band played two cubic Zumba "Cabaret" Concert	/CWD
			party gave performance to the Men of the Battalion 22nd	/CWD
			which drive given for benefit of the Men. Surrey to month	/CWD
			there Other ranks were demobilized.	/CWD

W.S. Nicholson. Lt.Col.
Commanding 11th Cameron Hrs

A.Gs. No. AG/2158/9113 (O)
40th Division No. 23 (A)
120th Inf. Bde. No. 120/400.

Headquarters,
　Cavalry Corps 'A'

　　　In confirmation of my wire AF889 of 4/2/19, will you kindly order Captain W.H.M.NICHOLLS, 20th Hussars, to proceed and report to Headquarters, 40th Division, for Command of an Infantry Battalion.

　　　Date of departure to be reported.

G.H.Q.　　　　　　　　　　(sgd) E.GLADSTONE, Captain, S.C.
5/2/19.　　　　　　　　　　　　　for Adjutant-General

　　　　　　　　　(2)

Headquarters,
　120th Infantry Brigade.

　　　For your information.

　　　On arrival this officer will be sent to take Command of the 11th Bn. Cameron Highlanders, vice Lt-Col. Hon. O.R.VIVIAN, M.V.O., D.S.O.

　　　Date of assuming duties to be reported to this office.

　　　　　　　　　(3)

O.C. 11th Bn. Cameron Highlanders.

　　　For information.

　　　　　　　　　　　　　　　　(signature)
　　　　　　　　　　　　　　　　　　　Captain,
　　　　　　　　　　　　　　　　　　Staff Captain,
　　　　　　　　　　　　　　　　120th Infantry Brigade.

9/2/19.

40th Div.
120th Bde.

WAR DIARY

11th BATTN. CAMERON HLDRS.

MAY
1919.

WAR DIARY of 1/11th Batt. Cameron Hrs
May 1919
Volume I

Army Form C. 2118

Page 40

Page I INTELLIGENCE SUMMARY
(Erase heading not required.)

Place	Date	Hour	Summary of Events and Information	Remarks and references to Appendices
CROIX	1/5/19		2/5/19 Trip to Brussels and Zeebrugge lasting 2 days for the benefit of the men. 6/5/19 Church service held. 11/5/19 Divisional sports held. Croix Civilian fatigue post in Croix abs. 10 O.R. 6 O.R. left from making cadre 35" O.Rs. 13/5/19 Church service held. 23/5/19 All Transport concentrate on Railhead siding, in preparation for move of Cadre to England. 24/5/19 Transport loaded on train and entrained of Cadre. 25/5/19 Arrived Dunkirk 1 a.m. Slept in train moved into No 3 Camp at Malo yk Bol. after men having their bath and clean change of clothing. 26/5/19 – 30/5/19. Entrained at No 3 Camp's where short was indulged in. 30/5/19 Sailed on S.S. Clutha for Southampton, arriving Southampton 6 a.m. 31/5/19. Loading train & detraining on final stage of the journey at 12 midday. 1/6/19. The Colours preceded & conducted to Bathurst being inspected the necessary escort the journey through.	

W.M.Nicholls Lieut Col
Commdg 1/11 Cameron Hrs

www.ingramcontent.com/pod-product-compliance
Lightning Source LLC
Chambersburg PA
CBHW081238170426

43191CB00034B/1974